PINE HILLS BRANCH
ALBANY PUBLIC LIBRARY

THE PRISONER OF ZENDA

Rudolf Rassendyll is young, rich, and comes from an old English family. But he has the dark red hair and the long straight nose of the royal family of Ruritania – the result of a little family 'accident' many years before.

Rudolf decides to visit Ruritania for the coronation of the new king. He arrives in the town of Zenda and goes for a quiet walk in the forest. By the next morning he is in the middle of adventures beyond his wildest dreams. With his new friends, Captain Sapt and Fritz von Tarlenheim, he is making plans to rescue the prisoner in the Castle of Zenda. Soon he is fighting the King's enemies, Black Michael the Duke, and Rupert of Hentzau – and falling in love with the King's cousin, the lovely Princess Flavia.

And the King . . . But who *is* the King of Ruritania?

D1169793

PINE HILLS BRANCH
ALBANY PUBLIC LIBRARY

OXFORD BOOKWORMS LIBRARY
Thriller & Adventure

The Prisoner of Zenda

Stage 3 (1000 headwords)

Series Editor: Jennifer Bassett
Founder Editor: Tricia Hedge
Activities Editors: Jennifer Bassett and Alison Baxter

ANTHONY HOPE

The Prisoner of Zenda

Retold by
Diane Mowat

Illustrated by
Alan Marks

OXFORD UNIVERSITY PRESS

OXFORD
UNIVERSITY PRESS

Great Clarendon Street, Oxford OX2 6DP

Oxford University Press is a department of the University of Oxford
It furthers the University's objective of excellence in research, scholarship,
and education by publishing worldwide in

Oxford New York

Auckland Bangkok Buenos Aires Cape Town Chennai
Dar es Salaam Delhi Hong Kong Istanbul Karachi Kolkata
Kuala Lumpur Madrid Melbourne Mexico City Mumbai Nairobi
São Paulo Shanghai Taipei Tokyo Toronto

Oxford and Oxford English are registered trade marks of
Oxford University Press in the UK and in certain other countries

ISBN 0 19 423012 0

This simplified edition © Oxford University Press 2000

Sixth impression 2003

First published in Oxford Bookworms 1993
This second edition published in the Oxford Bookworms Library 2000

A complete recording of this Bookworms edition of *The Prisoner of Zenda*
is available on cassette ISBN 0 19 422778 2

No unauthorized photocopying

All rights reserved. No part of this publication may be reproduced,
stored in a retrieval system, or transmitted, in any form or by any
means, without the prior permission in writing of Oxford University
Press, or as expressly permitted by law, or under terms agreed
with the appropriate reprographics rights organization. Enquiries
concerning reproduction outside the scope of the above should
be sent to the ELT Rights Department, Oxford University Press,
at the address above

You must not circulate this book in any other binding or cover
and you must impose this same condition on any acquirer

Illustration on page 3 by Dave Murray

Typeset by Wyvern Typesetting Ltd, Bristol
Printed in Spain by Unigraf s.l.

CONTENTS

1

The Rassendylls – and the Elphbergs

'I wonder when you're going to do something useful, Rudolf,' my brother's wife said. She looked at me crossly over the breakfast table.

'But why should I do anything, Rose?' I answered, calmly eating my egg. 'I've got nearly enough money for the things I want, and my brother, Robert, is a lord – Lord Burlesdon. I'm very happy.'

'You're twenty-nine, and you've done nothing except . . .'

'Play about? It's true. We Rassendylls are a rich and famous family, and we don't need to do anything.'

'We Rassendylls don't need to do anything,' I said.

1

This made Rose angry. 'Rich and famous families usually behave worse than less important families,' she said.

When I heard this, I touched my dark red hair. I knew what she meant.

'I'm so pleased that Robert's hair is black!' she cried.

Just then my brother, Robert, came in. When he looked at Rose, he could see that there was something wrong.

'What's the matter, my dear?' he said.

'Oh, she's angry because I never do anything useful, and because I've got red hair,' I said.

'Well, I know he can't do much about his hair, or his nose . . .' Rose began.

'No, the nose and the hair are in the family,' my brother agreed. 'And Rudolf has both of them.'

In the room there were many family pictures, and one of them was of a very beautiful woman, Lady Amelia, who lived a hundred and fifty years ago. I stood up and turned to look at it.

'If you took that picture away, Robert,' Rose cried, 'we could forget all about it.'

'Oh, but I don't want to forget about it,' I replied. 'I like being an Elphberg.'

But perhaps I should stop for a moment and explain why Rose was angry about my nose and my hair – and why I, a Rassendyll, said I was an Elphberg. After all, the Elphbergs are the royal family of Ruritania, and have been for hundreds of years.

The story is told in a book about the Rassendyll family history.

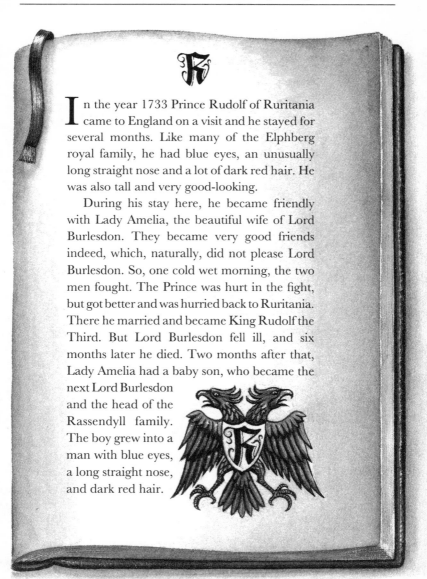

In the year 1733 Prince Rudolf of Ruritania came to England on a visit and he stayed for several months. Like many of the Elphberg royal family, he had blue eyes, an unusually long straight nose and a lot of dark red hair. He was also tall and very good-looking.

During his stay here, he became friendly with Lady Amelia, the beautiful wife of Lord Burlesdon. They became very good friends indeed, which, naturally, did not please Lord Burlesdon. So, one cold wet morning, the two men fought. The Prince was hurt in the fight, but got better and was hurried back to Ruritania. There he married and became King Rudolf the Third. But Lord Burlesdon fell ill, and six months later he died. Two months after that, Lady Amelia had a baby son, who became the next Lord Burlesdon and the head of the Rassendyll family. The boy grew into a man with blue eyes, a long straight nose, and dark red hair.

3

These things can happen in the best of families, and among the many pictures of the Rassendylls at home, you can see that five or six of them have the same blue eyes, the same nose, and the same red hair.

So, because my hair was red and I had the Elphberg nose, Rose worried about me. In the end, to please her, I promised to get a job in six months' time. This gave me six free months to enjoy myself first.

And an idea came to me – I would visit Ruritania. None of my family had ever been there. They preferred to forget all about the Lady Amelia. But I saw in the newspaper that, in three weeks, the new young King, Rudolf the Fifth, would have his coronation. It would be an interesting time to visit the country.

I knew my family would not like my going, so I told them I was going walking in Austria.

2

The colour of men's hair

On the way to Ruritania I decided to spend a night in Paris with a friend. The next morning he came with me to the station, and as we waited for the train, we watched the crowds. We noticed a tall, dark, very fashionable lady, and my friend told me who she was.

'That's Madame Antoinette de Mauban.'

'That's Madame Antoinette de Mauban. She's travelling on the same train as you, but don't fall in love with her.'

'Why not?' I asked, amused.

'Ah,' said my friend, 'all Paris knows that she's in love with Duke Michael of Strelsau. And he, as you know, is the half-brother of the new King of Ruritania. Although he's only the second son and will never be king himself, he's still an important man and very popular, I hear, with many Ruritanians. The lovely Madame Antoinette won't look twice at you, Rudolf.'

I laughed, but he had woken my interest in the lady. I did not speak to her during the journey, and when we arrived in Ruritania, I left the train at Zenda, a small town outside the capital. But I noticed that Madame de Mauban went on to Strelsau, the capital.

5

I was welcomed very kindly at my hotel. It belonged to a fat old lady and her pretty daughter. From them I learned that the coronation was to be on the day after next, and not in three weeks.

The old lady was more interested in Duke Michael of Strelsau than in the new King. The Castle of Zenda and all the land around it belonged to the Duke, but the old lady said, 'It's not enough. Duke Michael should be king. He spends all his time with us. Every Ruritanian knows him, but we never see the new King.'

But the daughter cried, 'Oh no, I hate Black Michael. I want a red Elphberg – and the King, our friend Johann says, is very red. Johann works for the Duke and he's seen the King. In fact, the King's staying just outside Zenda now,' she added. 'He's resting at the Duke's house in the forest before going on to Strelsau on Wednesday for his coronation. The Duke's already in Strelsau, getting everything ready.'

'They're friends?' I asked.

'Friends who want the same place and the same wife,' the pretty girl replied. 'The Duke wants to marry his cousin, Princess Flavia, but people say she's going to be King Rudolf's wife and the Queen.'

Just then their friend, Johann, entered the room.

'We have a visitor, Johann,' the girl's mother said, and Johann turned towards me. But when he saw me, he stepped back, with a look of wonder on his face.

'What's the matter, Johann?' the daughter asked.

'Good evening, sir,' Johann said, still staring at me. He did not seem to like what he saw.

The girl began to laugh. 'It's the colour of your hair, sir,' she explained. 'We don't often see that colour here. It's the Elphberg red – not Johann's favourite colour.'

*

The next day I decided to walk through the forest for a few miles and take the train to Strelsau from a little station along the road. I sent my luggage on by train and after lunch, I started out on foot. First, I wanted to see the Castle of Zenda and in half an hour I had climbed the hill to it. There were two buildings – the old one, with a moat around it, and the new, modern building. Duke Michael could have friends to stay with him in the new castle, but he could go into the old castle when he wanted to be alone. The water in the moat was deep, and if he pulled up the drawbridge over the moat, no one could get to him.

The water in the moat was deep.

I stayed there for some time and looked at the castle, and then I walked on through the forest for about an hour. It was beautiful and I sat down to enjoy it. Before I knew what had happened, I was asleep.

Suddenly I heard a voice say, 'Good heavens! He looks just like the King!'

When I opened my eyes, there were two men in front of me. One of them came nearer.

'May I ask your name?' he said.

'Well, why don't you tell me your names first?' I replied.

The younger of the two men said, 'This is Captain Sapt, and I am Fritz von Tarlenheim. We work for the King of Ruritania.'

'And I am Rudolf Rassendyll,' I answered, 'a traveller from England. My brother is Lord Burlesdon.'

'Of course! The hair!' Sapt cried. 'You know the story, Fritz?'

Just then a voice called out from the trees behind us. 'Fritz! Fritz! Where are you, man?'

'It's the King!' Fritz said, and Sapt laughed.

Then a young man jumped out from behind a tree. I gave a cry, and when he saw me, he stepped back in sudden surprise. The King of Ruritania looked just like Rudolf Rassendyll, and Rudolf Rassendyll looked just like the King!

For a moment the King said nothing, but then he asked, 'Captain . . . Fritz . . . who is this?'

Sapt went to the King and spoke quietly in his ear. The King's surprise changed slowly to an amused smile, then suddenly he began to laugh loudly. 'Well met, cousin!'

he cried. 'Where are you travelling to?'

'To Strelsau, sir – to the coronation.'

The King looked at his friends, and, for a moment, he was serious. But then he began to laugh again. 'Wait until brother Michael sees that there are two of us!' he cried.

'Perhaps it isn't a very good idea for Mr Rassendyll to go to Strelsau,' Fritz said, worried, and Sapt agreed with him.

'Oh, we'll think about the coronation tomorrow,' the King said. 'Tonight we'll enjoy ourselves. Come, cousin!'

We returned to the Duke's house in the forest, where we had an excellent dinner. The King called loudly for wine, and Captain Sapt and Fritz seemed worried. Clearly, the King liked his wine a little too much.

'Remember the coronation is tomorrow,' warned old Sapt.

The King liked his wine a little too much.

9

But the King was only interested in enjoying himself tonight, so we all drank and talked, and drank again. At last the King put down his glass and said, 'I've drunk enough.'

As he said that, old Josef, the King's servant, came in. He put some very special old wine on the table in front of the King and said, 'Duke Michael offers you this wine and asks you to drink it for love of him.'

'Well done, Black Michael!' the King cried. 'Well, I'm not afraid to drink your wine!'

And he drank every drop of wine in the bottle, himself. Then his head fell forward on to the table, and soon afterwards I too remembered no more of that wild evening.

3

The King goes to his coronation

I do not know how long I was asleep, but when I woke up I was cold and wet. Sapt and Fritz stood there looking at me. 'We had to wake you,' Sapt said. 'Cold water was the only way.'

Fritz took my arm and turned me round. 'Look!' he said.

The King was on the floor, and when Sapt pushed him with his foot, he did not move.

'We've been trying to wake him for half an hour,' said Fritz. 'But he's sleeping like a dead man.'

The three of us looked at each other.

'Was there something in that last bottle of wine?' I asked.

'I don't know,' Sapt said, 'but if he doesn't get to his coronation today, there'll never be a coronation for him. All Ruritania is waiting for him in Strelsau and Black Michael with half the army, too. We can't tell them that the King is too drunk to go to his own coronation!'

'You can say he's ill,' I said.

'Ill!' Sapt laughed angrily. 'Everybody will know what that means. He's been "ill" too many times before.'

'Tell me, do you think somebody put something in his wine?' I asked.

'It was Black Michael!' Fritz replied. 'We all know he wants to be King himself.'

For a moment or two we were all silent, and then Sapt looked at me, 'You must go to Strelsau and take his place!'

I stared at him. 'You're crazy, man! How can I do that? The King . . .'

'It's dangerous, I know,' said Sapt. 'But it's our only chance. If you don't go, Black Michael will be King and the real king will be dead or a prisoner.'

How could I refuse? It took me two minutes to decide.

'I'll go!' I said.

'Well done, boy!' cried Sapt. He went on quickly and quietly. 'After the coronation they'll take us to the palace for the night. When we're alone, you and I will leave and ride back here to fetch the King. He'll be all right by then. I'll take him back to Strelsau and you must get out of the country as fast as you can.'

11

'But what about the soldiers?' Fritz asked. 'They're Duke Michael's men, and they're coming to take the King back to Strelsau for the coronation.'

'We'll go before the soldiers get here,' Sapt said, 'and we'll hide the King.'

Sapt picked up the King in his arms.

He picked up the King in his arms and we opened the door. An old woman, Johann's mother, was standing there. She turned, without a word, and went back to the kitchen.

'Did she hear?' Fritz asked.

'Don't worry. I'll make sure she can't talk,' Sapt said, and he carried the King away.

When he returned, he told us that he had locked the old woman in a room underground. The King and Josef were hidden in another room underground. 'Josef will take care of the King and tell him everything when he wakes up. Come,' he went on, 'there's no time to lose. It's already six o'clock.'

Soon I was dressed in the King's clothes, the horses were ready and we were on our way. As we rode through the forest, Sapt told me everything that he could about my life, my family, my friends, and the things I liked or did not like. He told me what to do when we got there, and how to speak to different people. He was a wonderful teacher, and I listened hard. One mistake could mean death for all three of us.

It was eight o'clock when we arrived at the station and got on the train, and by half-past nine we were in Strelsau.

And when King Rudolf the Fifth stepped out of the train, the people shouted, 'God save the King!'

Old Sapt smiled, 'God save them both,' he said quietly. 'I only hope we are all alive tonight!'

4

My adventures begin

As we made our way to the palace, I began to feel that I really was the King of Ruritania, with Marshal Strakencz, the head of the army, on my right and old Sapt on my left. I could see that Strelsau was really two towns – the Old Town and the New Town. The people of the Old Town, who were poor, wanted Duke Michael to be their King, but the people of the New Town wanted King Rudolf. We went through the New Town first, and it was bright and colourful, with the ladies' dresses and the red roses of the Elphbergs. The people shouted loudly for their King as we passed through the streets. But when we came to the Old Town, the Marshal and Sapt moved nearer to my horse, and I could see that they were afraid for me.

'Stay back!' I called. 'I'll show my people that I'm not afraid of them.' Some of the crowd were pleased when they heard this, but most of them watched me in silence.

Finally, we reached the great church of Strelsau. I remember very little of the coronation – only two faces. One was a beautiful girl with wonderful red hair, the Princess Flavia. The other was the face of a man with black hair and dark, deep eyes – Black Michael. When he saw me, his face turned white. Clearly, he was surprised and deeply unhappy to see me.

The coronation seemed to last for hours, but I managed to

I remember very little of the coronation.

say and do all the right things. At last it was over, and I was now the King of Ruritania! As Princess Flavia and I drove back to the palace in an open car, one man in the crowd called out, 'When's the wedding?'

The Princess's face went a little pink when she heard this.

After a while she said, 'You seem different today, Rudolf. Quieter and more serious. Are you going to become a more sensible person now?'

The Princess, I realized, did not think very highly of the King. As for me, I thought the King was a very lucky man.

'If that will please you, I'll try to do it,' I said softly.

The Princess's face went pink again. Then she said, 'You must be careful of Michael. You know—'

'I know,' I said, 'that he wants what I have, and also what I hope to have one day.' As I spoke, I looked at her, and she smiled at me prettily.

'I wonder what the King's doing now,' I thought.

*

The royal dinner went on for a long time, but at last Fritz, Sapt, and I were alone in the King's dressing-room.

'You did well,' Fritz said, 'but, Rassendyll, be careful! Black Michael looked blacker than ever today – because you and the Princess had so much to say to each other.'

'She's very beautiful,' I replied.

'Come on,' Sapt cried. 'There's no time for that now. We must leave for Zenda at once, to find the King! If we're caught, we'll all be killed! Black Michael has had a letter from Zenda, so perhaps he knows already. Don't unlock the door, Fritz, while we're away, or you'll be a dead man. Say the King must be left alone to rest. Now, come on. The horses are ready.'

Fritz and I shook hands, then I covered my red hair and most of my face. Sapt and I left the room by a secret door, and we found ourselves outside, at the back of the palace gardens.

A man was waiting there with two horses.

Soon we left the town behind us, and we were out in the country. We rode like the wind and by ten o'clock had come to the edge of the forest of Zenda.

Suddenly Sapt stopped. 'Listen!' he said quietly. 'Horses behind us! Quick! Get down! The castle's to the left,' he continued. 'Our road's to the right.'

We hid in the thick trees, and we waited and watched. The men came nearer. It was Black Michael and another man. When they came to the two roads, they stopped.

It was Black Michael and another man.

'Which way?' the Duke asked.

'To the castle!' the other man cried. 'They'll know there what's been happening.'

The Duke waited for a moment. 'To Zenda then!' he cried finally, and the two men took the road to the left.

We waited for ten more minutes, and then we hurried on.

When we arrived at the house in the forest, we ran to the underground rooms. The one where Sapt had locked up the old woman was empty. She had escaped! The other room was locked. Sapt's face was white with fear. Between us, we broke down the door and ran in. I found a light and looked round the room. The servant Josef was on the floor – dead! I held up the light and looked in every corner of the room.

'The King isn't here!' I said.

5

His Majesty returns to Strelsau

It was one o'clock in the morning. For a few minutes we said nothing. Then Sapt cried, 'The Duke's men have taken the King prisoner!'

'Then we must get back and wake everyone in Strelsau!' I cried. 'We must catch Black Michael before he kills the King.'

'Who knows where the King is now?' Sapt answered. Then suddenly he began to laugh. 'But we've given Black

Michael a problem,' he said. 'Yes, my boy. We'll go back to Strelsau. The King will be in his palace in Strelsau again tomorrow.'

'No!' I cried.

'Yes!' Sapt answered. 'It's the only way to help him. Go back and take his place for him.'

'But the Duke knows . . .'

'Yes, but he can't speak, can he? What can he say? "This man isn't the King because I've taken the real King prisoner and murdered his servant." Can he say that?'

'But people will soon realize I'm not the real King,' I said.

'Perhaps, perhaps not,' said Sapt. 'But we must have a King in Strelsau, or Michael will ride in tomorrow as the new King! Listen, boy, if you don't go back to Strelsau, they'll kill the King. And if you *do* go back, they *can't* kill the King. Because if they kill him, how can they ever say that you're not the real King? Don't you see?' he cried. 'It's a dangerous game, but it gives us a chance of winning.'

It was a wild, hopeless plan, but I was young. I would never have the chance of an adventure like this again. 'Sapt, I'll try it,' I said.

'Good for you!' Sapt cried. 'But we must hurry! Look!'

He pulled me over to the door. The moon was low now, and there was not much light, but I could just see a small group of men on horses. They were Black Michael's men, probably coming to take the dead body of Josef away.

'We can't let them go without doing something,' I said, thinking of poor Josef.

'Right,' Sapt agreed. We ran out of the back of the house, and quickly got onto our horses. Silently, we waited in the darkness, and then we galloped round the house and straight into the group of men. Between us, we killed three of them, but a bullet hit my finger and it began to bleed.

We galloped straight into the group of men.

We rode hard all night and it was about eight or nine o'clock in the morning when we reached Strelsau. Luckily, the streets were still empty. We arrived at the palace, went in, and got to the dressing-room. When we opened the door, Fritz was asleep, but he woke immediately. When he saw me, he fell to the ground and cried, 'Thank God, Your Majesty! You're safe!'

'Well done, boy!' Sapt shouted. 'We'll do it!'

Fritz stood up. He looked at me, up and down, down and up. Then he took a step backwards. 'Where's the King?' he cried.

'Be quiet,' Sapt warned him. 'Someone will hear!'

Fritz's face was white now. 'Is the King dead?' he asked quietly.

'Please God, no,' I answered. 'But Black Michael has him.'

*

The next day was a long one for me. Sapt talked to me for three hours about what I must do and what I must say, what I liked and what I didn't like. Then I had to do some of the King's business, but, because of my damaged finger, I did not have to write my name on any papers.

When, at last, I was alone with Sapt and Fritz, we began to talk about Black Michael. Fritz told me that Black Michael had six very dangerous men among his servants – three Ruritanians, a Belgian, a Frenchman, and an Englishman. They did anything that the Duke ordered, and did not stop at murder. Three of them – the foreigners, Fritz had heard – were in Strelsau now with Duke Michael.

Sapt banged the table with his hand in excitement. 'Then the King must be alive! Michael's brought the foreigners with him, and left the three Ruritanians to hold the King prisoner. Usually, the Six, as they're called, go everywhere with him.'

Fritz wanted to do something immediately about Black Michael and his men, but Sapt and I realized that we could not do anything openly.

'We'll play a waiting game, and let Michael make the first move,' I said.

And so I continued as King of Ruritania. In order to help the real King, I tried to make myself popular with the people. I went riding through the streets, smiling and talking to everybody. I also went to visit the Princess Flavia. The King's officials had told me that the Princess was very popular, and the people hoped that she would become my wife.

It was easy for me to pretend to be in love with the Princess.

We sat together for a long time, talking of this and that.

Too easy. Those beautiful eyes and that lovely smile were stealing my heart. Here was my greatest danger! I was pretending to be another man, but losing my own heart. On my first visit, we sat together for a long time, talking of this and that. When I got up to leave, Princess Flavia said, 'Rudolf, you will be careful, won't you? You have enemies, as I'm sure you know, and your life is very important to . . . Ruritania.'

'Only to Ruritania?' I asked softly.

'And to your loving cousin,' she answered quietly.

I could not speak. I took her hand in mine. Then, with a heavy heart, I left.

Of course, I made many mistakes in my new life as King. But I managed to talk my way out of them, with luck and with help from Fritz and Sapt. It was like living on a knife edge. Once I met my brother Michael in the Princess's house. We smiled and talked politely, but I could see the anger in his black eyes.

6

An adventure with a tea-table

One day Sapt brought me some news – he had found out where the King was. Duke Michael was holding him prisoner somewhere in the Castle of Zenda.

Sapt also brought me a letter. It was in a woman's handwriting.

'To know what you most wish to know,' the letter began, 'meet me tonight in the garden of the big house in New Avenue. Come at midnight, and come alone.'

There was another note on the back of the letter. 'Ask yourself which woman does not want Black Michael to marry the Princess. A. de M.'

'Antoinette de Mauban!' I cried. '*She* wants to marry the Duke.'

'That's true,' Sapt said. 'But you won't go, of course. They'll kill you! Duke Michael made her write this letter!'

'I must,' I replied. 'Every day we play this game there's more danger. I could make a mistake at any time, and, if I do, we'll all die. Don't you see? I have to go tonight. We can't go on much longer.'

'Then I'm coming too,' said Sapt.

So, at half-past eleven that night, Sapt and I rode out to the house in New Avenue. We left Fritz to watch my room in the palace. The night was dark, so I took a lamp. I also had my revolver and a knife.

We soon reached the house, and came to a gate in the wall. I got off my horse.

'I'll wait here,' said Sapt. 'If I hear anything, I'll—'

'Stay where you are!' I answered quickly. 'It's the King's only chance. They mustn't kill you too!'

'You're right,' said Sapt. 'Good luck!'

Silently, I opened the gate and went into the garden. In front of me I could see the dark shape of a summer-house and I moved towards it. Without a sound, I went up the steps,

24

Silently, I opened the gate and went into the garden.

pushed open the door and went in. A woman hurried over to me and took me by the hand. I turned my lamp on her. She was beautiful.

'Close the door!' she said. 'We must be quick, Mr Rassendyll! Michael made me write the letter – three men are coming to kill you – three of the Six! They'll tell everyone that Sapt and Fritz von Tarlenheim murdered you. Then Michael will make himself King and marry the Princess.' Antoinette's beautiful eyes were sad as she added softly, 'I can't let him marry her. I love him!'

'But the King,' I said. 'I know he's in the Castle of Zenda – but where?'

'Go across the drawbridge and you come to a heavy door . . . Listen! What's that? They're coming! They're too soon! Put out your lamp!' she cried, her eyes filled with fear. 'Quickly! You must go. There's a ladder at the end of the garden, against the wall!'

But it was too late. The three men were already outside. There was a small hole in the door, and I put my eye to it. My hand was on my revolver. It was no good! There were three of them. I could kill one perhaps, but then . . .

A voice came from outside. 'Mr Rassendyll . . .' It was the Englishman. 'We only want to talk to you. Open the door.'

'We can talk through the door,' I replied. I looked through the hole again and saw that they were on the top step. When I opened the door, they would run at me.

'We'll let you go if you leave the country and we'll give you fifty thousand English pounds,' continued Detchard, the Englishman.

'Give me a minute to think,' I answered.

Wildly, I looked around the summer-house and saw a metal garden table and some chairs. I picked up the table and held it in front of me, by the legs. Then I went to the back of the room and waited.

'All right, I agree,' I called. 'Open the door!'

I heard them arguing with each other, and then Detchard said to the Belgian, 'Why, Bersonin, are you afraid of one man?'

A second later the door opened.

I held the table in front of me, by the legs.

De Gautet, the Frenchman, was with the other two, and the three men were standing there with their revolvers ready. With a shout, I ran at them as hard as I could. They tried to shoot me, but the bullets hit the table. The next second the table knocked them to the ground and we all fell on top of each other. Quickly, I picked myself up and ran for my life through the trees. I could hear them coming after me. Was Antoinette right? Was there really a ladder by the wall? I reached the end of the garden. The ladder was there! In a minute I was up it and over the wall.

Sapt was waiting with the horses and seconds later we were on our way home. And, as we rode, we laughed because I had fought Duke Michael's dangerous men – with a tea-table!

In a minute I was up the ladder and over the wall.

7

For love of the King

Every day I was sent a secret report by the Chief of Police, and the next afternoon I was playing cards with Fritz when Sapt brought it in. We learned that Duke Michael and the Three had left Strelsau, and that Antoinette de Mauban had also left. Clearly, they had gone to Zenda. The report also said that the people were unhappy because the King had not yet asked Princess Flavia to marry him.

'Yes,' said Fritz. 'It's true. I've heard that the Princess loves the King and she's very sad . . .'

'Well,' Sapt informed us, 'I've arranged a dance at the royal palace this evening, for the Princess.'

'Why wasn't I told?' I asked angrily.

But Sapt continued, 'Everything is arranged. And tonight you must ask the Princess to marry you.'

'No! I'll do nothing to hurt her!' I cried.

'All right, my boy,' Sapt smiled gently. 'Just say something nice to her, then. Remember, she thinks you're the King and we don't want her to be angry with him, do we?'

I understood, of course. If the King was saved, then Flavia must marry him. If he was not saved, then Sapt would ask me to stay and marry the Princess. Duke Michael must not be King.

The dance was wonderful. Flavia was beautiful and I danced with her again and again. Everyone could feel our happiness. I forgot about the crowd of rich, colourful people who were watching us. I had eyes only for my beautiful Flavia.

When supper had finished, Fritz touched me on the shoulder. I stood up, took Flavia's hand and led her into a little room. They brought coffee to us and then the door was closed quietly. The Princess and I were alone.

The windows of the little room opened onto the garden. The night was fine and the room was filled with the sweet smell of the flowers outside. Flavia sat down and I stood opposite her. I was fighting with myself . . . But then she looked at me – and I was lost! I forgot the King, I forgot who I was, I forgot everything! I fell to my knees, took her gently in my arms and kissed her.

I took Flavia gently in my arms and kissed her.

30

Suddenly she pushed me away. 'Is it true? Do you really love me?' she cried. 'Or is it because you're the King and you must marry me?'

'No!' I answered quietly. 'I love you more than my life!'

Flavia smiled. 'Oh, why do I love you now?' she said softly. 'I didn't love you before, but I do now.'

How happy I was! It was not the King she loved. It was me – it was Rudolf Rassendyll! But as I looked into her lovely face, I knew I could not live with the lie. How could I pretend to be the King any longer?

'There's something I must tell you . . .' I began in a low voice.

'Your Majesty,' said a voice from the garden. 'People are waiting to say goodbye.'

It was Sapt. He had heard me talking to the Princess.

'We'll come,' I replied coldly.

But Flavia, her eyes full of her love for me, held out her hand to Sapt as he came into the room. He took it and said softly and sadly, 'God save your Royal Highness.' And then he added, 'But before all comes the King – God save the King!'

When Sapt told the people that Princess Flavia had accepted the King as her future husband, they were wild with happiness.

'You know, Sapt,' I said sadly, 'I could marry the Princess and let my people kill Duke Michael – and the King.'

'I know,' Sapt replied quietly.

'So we must go to Zenda and bring the King home at once!' I said.

31

'You're the finest Elphberg of them all,' said Sapt.

Sapt put his hand on my shoulder. 'You're the finest Elphberg of them all,' he said with feeling.

*

Before we left Strelsau, I saw the Marshal and asked him to stay near Flavia, to take care of her and to keep her safe from Duke Michael. Then I went to say goodbye to her. At first she was cold with me. She did not understand why I wanted to leave her. But her anger changed to fear when I told her that I was going after Duke Michael.

'Oh, Rudolf, be careful!' she cried. 'He's a dangerous man! Please come back safely to me.'

'Duke Michael can never keep me away from you,' I promised. But in my heart I knew that another man could.

8

Back to Zenda

The next day Sapt, Fritz, and I left Strelsau to go to Tarlenheim House. This fine modern house belonged to Fritz's uncle and was near the Castle of Zenda. We had ten brave young men with us. Sapt had told them that a friend of the King's was a prisoner in the Castle of Zenda and that the King needed their help.

Michael, of course, knew of my arrival. But I was sure he did not understand why I had come. He would think that my plan was to kill him *and* the King – and marry the Princess myself. So, I had not been in the house an hour when he sent three of the Six to me. These were not the three men who had tried to kill me. This time he sent the three Ruritanians – Lauengram, Krafstein and young Rupert of Hentzau.

'Duke Michael is very sorry that he can't welcome you himself,' explained Rupert of Hentzau. 'But, sadly, he's ill at the moment.'

'I hope that my dear brother will soon be better,' I replied with a smile.

Rupert threw back his head, shook his black hair and laughed. He was a good-looking young man. People said he had broken many hearts already.

'Oh, I'm sure he will!' he answered.

*

Rupert threw back his head and laughed.

That evening, instead of having dinner at the house, Fritz and I went to the little hotel in the town of Zenda where I had stayed before.

'Ask for a room where we can dine alone,' I said to Fritz. 'And ask the pretty girl to bring our food.'

I covered my face and the girl came and put the wine down on the table. When she turned to go, she looked at me and I let her see my face.

'The King!' she cried. 'You were the King! Oh, I'm sorry, sir! I'm sorry! The things that we said!'

'Forget that now,' I answered. 'You can help me. Bring our dinner, but tell no one that the King is here.'

She came back in a few minutes, looking very serious.

'How's your friend Johann?' I began.

She looked surprised. 'Oh, we don't see him very often now,' she answered. 'He's very busy at the castle.'

'But you could get Johann to meet you tomorrow night, couldn't you? At ten o'clock, perhaps, on the road out of Zenda.'

'Yes, sir . . . You're not going to hurt him?'

'Not if he does what I say. Go now, and say nothing about this.'

After dinner, we left to go back to Tarlenheim House. We had almost reached it when we saw Sapt running to meet us. 'Have you seen them?' he cried.

'Who?' I asked.

'Duke Michael's men. Don't go out unless you have six men or more with you!' he said. 'You know Bernenstein, one of your men?'

'Of course,' I answered. 'A good, strong man, about as tall as me.'

'Well, they tried to kill him. He's upstairs now with a bullet in his arm. He was walking in the woods and he saw three men. Suddenly, they started shooting at him, so he began to run. He was lucky. They were afraid to come too near the house, so he escaped. But it was you they wanted to kill!'

'Sapt,' I said, 'I promise I'll do one thing for Ruritania before I leave it.'

'What's that?' asked Sapt.

'I'll kill every one of the Six. Ruritania will be a better place without them!'

9

News of the prisoner

The next morning I was sitting in the garden in the sun when suddenly I saw young Rupert of Hentzau on horseback coming through the trees towards me. He was not afraid of my men, but asked to speak with me alone. He said he had a message for me from the Duke of Strelsau. I asked my friends to move away, and Rupert came and sat down near me.

'Rassendyll,' he began, 'the Duke . . .'

'Don't you know how to speak to the King?' I asked.

'Why pretend with me?'

'Because it isn't finished yet.'

'Well, I'm here because I want to help you . . .'

'Then give me the message. What does the Duke want?' I asked.

'He wants you to leave. He'll take you safely out of the country and give you a hundred thousand pounds.'

'I refuse,' I replied immediately.

Rupert laughed. 'I knew it!' he cried. 'Duke Michael doesn't understand men like us! . . . You must die, then,' he added carelessly.

'Yes,' I answered. 'But you won't be alive to see me die!' I laughed. 'How's your prisoner?' I added.

'Alive,' he replied. 'How's the pretty Princess?'

I took a step towards him. 'Go now, before I kill you,' I shouted angrily.

Rupert turned, but suddenly he came back. He put out his right hand. 'Shake hands!' he called.

Of course, he knew what I would do. I put my hands behind my back. Quickly, his left hand moved towards me. In it he held a dagger and it was coming straight at my heart! I jumped to one side, and the dagger went deep into my shoulder. Before my friends could do anything, Rupert of Hentzau was on his horse and galloping through the trees. I heard my men going after him with their guns – and then everything went black.

The dagger went deep into my shoulder.

When I awoke it was dark, and Fritz was at my bedside. He told me that I was not badly hurt, and that the plan to catch Johann had been successful.

'He seems pleased to be here,' Fritz said. 'I think he's afraid of Duke Michael.'

Later Sapt brought Johann up to see me. At first Johann was afraid to speak, but then he began to talk. We asked him many questions, and finally Johann gave us the information we wanted.

In the Castle of Zenda, near the drawbridge and below the ground, there were two small rooms, cut out of the rock itself. In the first of these rooms there were always three of the Six. At the back of this room there was a door which led into the second room. The King was in the second room.

'If someone tries to get into the first room, two of the three men will fight, but Rupert of Hentzau or Detchard will run into the second room and kill the King,' Johann said. 'There's a small window in the second room with a large pipe going down into the moat outside,' he went on. 'You can get a man inside it, and they'll tie a heavy stone to the King's body and push it down the pipe. The body will go down and disappear under the water, and the murderers will then go down the pipe themselves, and swim across the moat.'

'There's a large pipe going down into the moat outside.'

38

'And if I bring an army to the castle?' I asked.

'Duke Michael will still murder the King,' replied Johann. 'He won't fight. He'll kill the King and push his body down the pipe. And he'll put one of the Six in the prison. He'll say the man had done something to make him angry. That will stop the stories about a prisoner in Zenda.' Johann stopped for a minute, but then he added, 'If they know I've told you this, they'll kill me. They're all bad, but Rupert of Hentzau is the worst. Don't let them kill me . . .'

'All right,' I said. 'But if anyone asks you who the prisoner of Zenda is, don't tell him. If you do, I'll kill you myself!'

Johann left the room and I looked at Sapt.

'It doesn't matter what plan we make,' I said. 'The King will be dead before we can get to him!'

Sapt shook his grey head angrily. 'You'll still be King of Ruritania in a year's time.'

'Perhaps one of the Duke's men will turn against him . . .' I began.

'Impossible,' replied Sapt.

'Then we need the help of God,' I said.

10

A night outside the castle

I wanted Duke Michael to think that I was still very ill, so we told the newspapers that the King had had a very serious accident. When Princess Flavia read this, she was very worried and she decided to come and see me. The Marshal could not stop her, and, although I was afraid for her, I was excited at the thought of seeing her again. We spent two wonderfully happy days together.

We had sent Johann back to the Castle of Zenda and suddenly we had a message from him. The real King was very ill.

'I must save him,' I said to myself. 'I love Flavia more each day. I can't go on like this much longer.'

I talked to Sapt. He agreed, so we made our plans.

*

Late the next night, Sapt, Fritz, and I, with six more men, rode out towards the Castle of Zenda. Sapt was carrying a long rope and I had a short, thick stick and a long knife.

The night was dark, and it was wet and windy. We stayed away from the town and we met no one. When we came to the moat, we stopped near some trees and the six men hid there with the horses. Then Sapt tied the rope round one of the trees near the water. I pulled off my boots, put the stick between my teeth and gently went down the rope into the water. I was going to take a look at the pipe.

I went down the rope into the water.

It had been warm and bright that day, and the water was not cold. Slowly and carefully I swam round the dark walls of the castle. There were lights in the new buildings, and from time to time I heard people shouting and laughing. 'That must be young Rupert and his friends,' I thought. Suddenly a dark shape appeared in front of me. It was the pipe! The bottom of it was very wide and came out into the moat. And then I saw something which nearly made my heart stop. It was a boat, and in the boat there was a man! His gun was beside him, but, luckily, he was asleep. As quietly as I could, I moved closer.

41

The man still slept. What could I do? I had to save the King. I took out my knife and drove it through the sleeping man's heart! On the other side of the castle they were still singing.

I had very little time. Someone could come at any minute. I looked up at where the pipe went through the wall into the prison. There was a thin line of light at the bottom edge. I heard Detchard's voice, and then I heard the King reply. Just then the light went out, and, in the darkness, I heard the King crying. I did not call to him. I had to get away safely – and take the body of the dead watchman with me.

I climbed into the boat and began to go back to where my friends were. No one could hear me because the wind was strong. But from somewhere behind me, I heard a shout. Someone was calling to the watchman. I reached the side of the moat where Sapt and Fritz were waiting. Quickly, I tied the rope round the man's body and Sapt and Fritz pulled it up. Then I climbed up the rope myself.

'Call our men from the trees,' I said quietly. 'And hurry!'

But just then, three men rode round from the front of the castle. Luckily, they did not see us, but they heard our six friends riding out of the trees, and with a shout they galloped towards them.

Seconds later we heard the sound of shots and I ran to help our men. Sapt and Fritz followed.

'Kill them!' cried a voice. It was Rupert of Hentzau.

'Too late! They've got both of us!' cried another voice. 'Save yourself, Rupert!'

I ran on, holding my stick in my hand. Suddenly, through

I jumped at the horse's head, and saw the man's face above me.

the darkness, I saw a horse coming towards me. I jumped at
the horse's head, and saw the man's face above me.

'At last!' I shouted. 'Rupert of Hentzau!'

He had only his sword, and my men were coming at him
from one side, and Sapt and Fritz from the other.

Rupert laughed. 'It's the play-actor!' he cried, and with his
sword he knocked my stick from my hand. Then he turned his
horse, galloped to the moat, and jumped into the water with
our bullets flying round his ears. Our men tried to shoot him

43

in the water, but it was dark, there was no moon – and we lost him.

We had killed two of the Six – Lauengram and Krafstein – but I was angry. Three of our brave friends were also dead, and we carried them home with a heavy heart.

And I did not like to hear Rupert call me a play-actor.

*

Of course, Michael and I could not let the people know that we were enemies. So, in the daytime it was safe to be in the town of Zenda. One day, soon after our night outside the castle, Princess Flavia and I were riding through the town when we saw a group of people dressed in black going to the church. Rupert of Hentzau was with them, and when he saw us, he turned his horse and came towards us.

'It's the funeral of my dear friend, Lauengram,' he said, in answer to our question.

'I'm sorry your friend is dead,' I said to him.

'And I'm sorry, too,' Flavia added, her beautiful blue eyes sad.

Rupert looked at her and smiled. Then he turned and rode away. Although I was angry because he had smiled at Flavia, I went after him.

'You fought bravely the other night,' I said, 'and you're young. Help me save the King – and I'll help you.'

But Rupert was not interested. 'No,' he answered. 'But if they were both dead – the King and the Duke – then you could be King and marry your Princess, and I could be rich, and have the woman I want.'

'And I could be rich,' said Rupert, 'and have the woman I want.'

'Antoinette de Mauban?' I asked carelessly, trying not to show my interest.

'Yes,' replied Rupert. 'I hate the Duke. She loves him, not me!' Angrily, he joined the funeral group again.

Strangely, when we returned home there was a message for me from Antoinette herself.

'I helped you once. Help me now. Save me from this terrible place! Save me from these murderers!'

I was sorry for her, but what could I do?

11

A dangerous plan

One day Johann came to tell us that the King was now very sick, and that Antoinette de Mauban and a doctor were looking after him. But the Duke never left Rupert of Hentzau alone with Antoinette. I understood why, after what Rupert had told me. There were often angry voices in the castle these days, Johann told us.

Two of the Six were now dead, but there were always two men watching the King. The other two slept in a room above and would hear them if they called. Detchard and Bersonin watched by night; Rupert of Hentzau and De Gautet by day. The Duke's rooms were on the first floor, in the new buildings of the castle, and Antoinette's room was on the same floor. But at night the Duke locked the door of her room, and pulled up the drawbridge. He kept the key himself. Johann slept near the front door of the new castle with five other men – but they had no guns.

We could not wait any longer. 'Listen!' I said to Johann. 'I'll make you rich if you do what I say.' Johann agreed.

'You must take this note to Madame de Mauban,' I said, 'and tomorrow, at two o'clock in the morning, you must open the front door of the new castle. Tell the others that you need air, or something – and then escape.'

Johann was clearly afraid, but he seemed to understand. I explained my plan to Sapt and Fritz.

'When Johann opens the front door,' I said, 'Sapt and his men will run into the castle and hold the men who are sleeping there. At the same time Antoinette will scream loudly again and again. She'll cry "Help! Help me, Michael!" And she'll shout Rupert of Hentzau's name. Duke Michael will hear and he'll run out of his room – straight into the hands of Sapt! Sapt will get the key from the Duke and let down the drawbridge. Rupert and De Gautet will hear the noise and hurry to cross the drawbridge. I'll hide by the bridge, in the moat, and when they try to cross, I'll kill them. Then we'll hurry to the room where the King is, and kill Detchard and Bersonin before they have time to kill the King.'

The others listened in silence. It was a very dangerous plan, and I did not really think it would work – but we had to try!

That evening I went to visit Flavia. She seemed very thoughtful, and as I was leaving, she placed a ring on my finger. I was wearing the King's ring, but I took off my Rassendyll family ring and gave it to her. 'Wear this for me always,' I said.

She kissed the ring, and replied seriously, 'I'll wear it until the day I die.'

And then I had to leave her. I had already told the Marshal that if anything happened to the King, he must take Flavia to Strelsau, tell the people that Duke Michael had killed the King – and that Flavia was their Queen. I knew this could be my last day alive.

'Wear this for me always.'

12

The prisoner and the King

We needed bad weather, but it was a fine, clear night. At midnight Sapt, Fritz, and their men left and rode quietly through the woods towards the castle. If everything went well, they would get there at a quarter to two and wait for Johann to open the front door. If Johann did not open the door, Fritz would come round to the other side of the castle to find me. If I was not there, then I was dead – and the King, too! Sapt and his men would go back to Tarlenheim House and return with the Marshal and more men to get into the castle.

So, half an hour later, I, too, left Tarlenheim. I took a shorter way than Sapt and when I reached the moat, I hid my horse in the trees, tied my rope round a strong tree and let myself down into the water. Slowly, I began to swim along under the castle walls. Just after a quarter to one, I came to the pipe and waited quietly in its shadow. Light was coming from Duke Michael's window opposite me across the moat, and I could see into the room. The next window along, which Johann had said was Antoinette's room, was dark.

Then the Duke's window opened, and Antoinette de Mauban looked out. Behind her there was a man. Rupert of Hentzau! What was he doing in the Duke's room? I wondered.

Rupert tried to put his arm round Antoinette, but she moved quickly away. At that moment, I heard the door of the room open and then the angry voice of Duke Michael.

'What are you doing here?' he cried.

'Waiting for you, sir,' Rupert replied quickly. 'I couldn't leave the lady alone.'

'Well, now you can go to bed. Are Detchard and Bersonin watching the prisoner?'

'Yes, sir.'

A few minutes later, Rupert crossed the drawbridge and it was pulled up. The light in Duke Michael's room went out, but a light came on, and stayed on, in Antoinette's room. In the silent darkness, I waited.

For about ten minutes everything was quiet, but suddenly I heard a noise on my side of the moat. A dark shape appeared in the gateway to the bridge, then turned and began to climb down some hidden steps in the wall. It was Rupert of Hentzau again – with a sword! Silently, he went down into the water

It was Rupert of Hentzau again – with a sword!

and swam across the moat. Then he climbed out, and I heard him unlock the door. It was clear that Rupert of Hentzau had his own secret plans for that night.

It was not yet time for Johann to open the front door for my friends, and I still had to wait. I climbed up to the gateway of the bridge and hid in a dark corner. Now no one could enter or leave the old castle without fighting me. I wondered what Rupert was doing now, and a few seconds later I found out.

There was a sudden crash, and then a woman's screams rang through the night.

'Help me, Michael! Rupert of Hentzau!'

Those were the words that I had written for Antoinette! But these were screams of real fear and soon I heard shouts and the sound of fighting from Antoinette's room. Then Rupert appeared at the window. His back was towards me, but he was fighting. 'That's for you, Johann,' I heard him cry. Then, 'Come on, Michael!'

So Johann was in there too, fighting at the Duke's side! How could he open the door for Sapt now?

More of the Duke's men had run to the room and the noise of the fighting grew louder. Suddenly, Rupert gave a wild laugh, and with his sword in his hand, jumped from the window into the moat below.

At that moment the door of the old castle opened and De Gautet appeared beside me. I jumped at him with my sword, and a second later he fell dead in the doorway without a word or a sound.

Wildly, I searched his body for the keys. I found them, and

in a minute I was in the first room, where Bersonin and Detchard were. But there was only Bersonin in the room. Before he had time to realize that I was there, I had killed him. Detchard had run into the King's room and locked the door behind him. I ran at it to break it down. But would I be in time? Was the King already dead?

The King was standing helplessly by the wall. But the doctor was also in the room and the brave little man had thrown himself at Detchard. He gave his life for the King, because, as I entered, Detchard pulled himself free and drove his sword into the doctor's side. Then, with an angry shout, Detchard turned to me.

With an angry shout, Detchard turned to me.

51

We fought long and hard. Detchard was an excellent swordsman, and I was growing tired. He drove me back against the wall, gave me a deep cut in the arm, and began to smile. In a second he would kill me.

Suddenly, the King realized who I was.

'Cousin Rudolf!' he cried. Then he picked up a chair and threw it at Detchard's legs. The Englishman, jumping to one side, turned his sword against the King, and with a cry the King fell to the ground. Detchard moved towards me again, stepped in the doctor's blood on the floor – and fell to the ground himself. I had him! A second later his body lay across the dead doctor.

But was the King dead? I had no time to find out, because just then I heard the noise of the drawbridge coming down. And that wild-cat Rupert of Hentzau was still alive. The King must wait for help while I fought his enemies. I ran out of the room and up the steps towards the drawbridge. And then I heard the sound of laughter – Rupert of Hentzau was laughing!

He was standing alone in the middle of the bridge. In the gateway on the far side stood a group of the Duke's men. They seemed too frightened to move.

'Come out, Michael, you dog!' Rupert shouted.

But a woman's wild cry answered him. 'He's dead! He's dead!'

The men in the gateway moved to one side and a woman came forward. Her face was as white as her long dress, and her dark hair lay over her shoulders. In her hand she held a gun. The shot rang out, but she missed. Rupert laughed. Again

Antoinette de Mauban faced him, her gun ready. But, before she could shoot, Rupert jumped over the side of the bridge, and down into the moat below.

Again, Antoinette de Mauban faced Rupert, her gun ready.

At that moment I heard the sound of running feet inside the new castle – and the welcome voice of my old friend, Captain Sapt! Then I knew that the King was safe and needed me no more. I ran out on to the bridge and jumped down into the moat. I had business to finish with Rupert of Hentzau.

*

I swam hard and caught up with him round the corner of the old castle. He had found my rope, climbed out of the moat, and was already running towards the trees where I had left my horse.

I ran after him as fast as I could. He turned and saw me, and called out, laughing, 'Why, it's the play-actor!' But then, with a cry of surprise, he found my horse, and in a minute he was on its back.

'Get down!' I shouted. 'Stand and fight, like a man!'

He turned, waiting for me, and I ran at him with my sword. For a few minutes we fought wildly. Blood ran from his face where I had cut it, but I had fought too many fights that night. He would surely kill me now.

I was saved by Fritz, who came galloping round the castle to find me. When Rupert saw him coming, he knew he had no chance.

'Goodbye, Rudolf Rassendyll!' he called. 'We'll meet again!'

And he rode away into the forest, laughing and singing . . . and still alive.

I fell to the ground. Blood was running again from the cut in my arm, and I could not stand. Fritz jumped down from his horse and lifted me in his arms.

And Rupert rode away into the forest, laughing and singing . . .

'Dear friend!' he said. 'Thank God I've found you! When Johann did not come, we had to break down the castle door. We were afraid we would be too late.'

'And the King . . .?' I said.

'Thanks to a very brave Englishman,' Fritz said gently, 'the King is alive.'

13

Goodbye to Ruritania

Old Sapt worked hard to keep our secret hidden. He sent messages, told lies, and gave orders. All his plans were successful, except one. Nothing can stop a woman in love.

'No!' cried Sapt. 'He is the man you love – but he is not the King!'

When Princess Flavia heard that the King was hurt, she refused to stay at Tarlenheim House and rode at once to the Castle of Zenda. Sapt had hidden me in a room in the old castle, and he and Fritz brought her to me there. How happy she was to see me! She threw her arms round my neck and kissed me.

'No!' cried Sapt. 'It's not the King. Don't kiss him. He is the man you love – but he is not the King!'

Flavia's face went white. 'What do you mean?' she cried. She turned to me again. 'Rudolf! Why do you let them say these things?'

I looked deeply into her eyes.

'It's true,' I said quietly. 'I am not the King.'

For a minute she continued to hold on to me. She looked at

56

Sapt, at Fritz, and finally at me again. Then, slowly, she fell forward and I laid her gently on the ground.

'I wish that Rupert had killed me,' I said.

*

I saw the King once more. He thanked me, and I gave him back the royal Elphberg ring. If he noticed Flavia's ring on my finger, he said nothing. We both knew that we would never meet again.

Before I left Ruritania, Princess Flavia asked to see me again, and Fritz took me to her. They had told her everything.

We had so much to say – and so little to say. A princess is not free to choose who to love.

'Flavia,' I said, 'I love you. I'll love you until the day I die.'

As I walked away, I heard her say my name again and again. 'Rudolf . . . Rudolf . . .' I can hear it now.

*

I live quietly now, but every year Fritz and I meet in a little town outside Ruritania. There, he gives me news of the Queen of Ruritania, the wife of King Rudolf the Fifth. And every year he brings me a red rose and a note with the words written: *Rudolf – Flavia – always*. And I send her a red rose with the same message.

Shall I ever see her again? Who knows?

GLOSSARY

behave to do things well or badly

coronation when someone is made a king or a queen

cousin the son or daughter of your aunt or uncle

dagger a sharp knife used for fighting

drawbridge a bridge across the moat of a castle, that can be
pulled up to stop people crossing

duke a title for an important nobleman

funeral when a dead person is put under the ground or is burned

Good heavens! an expression to show great surprise

Highness a word used when speaking to someone from a royal
family (*Your Royal Highness*)

kiss *(v)* to touch someone with your lips in a loving way

ladder two long pieces of wood with steps between them, used
for climbing up something

lead *(v)* to walk in front of someone to show them the way

lord a title for a nobleman (less important than a duke)

Majesty a word used when speaking to a king (*Your Majesty*),
or about a king (*His Majesty*)

Marshal a very important army officer

moat a deep wide ditch around a castle, filled with water

rescue *(v)* to save someone from danger

revolver a small gun, held in the hand

rope very strong, thick string

royal of a king or queen, or their family

servant someone who is paid to work in another person's house

shoulder the top of the arm where it joins the body

sword a long sharp knife (about a metre long), used for fighting

wine an alcoholic drink made from grapes

The Prisoner of Zenda

ACTIVITIES

Before Reading

1 **Read the story introduction on the first page of the book, and the back cover. What do you know now about Rudolf Rassendyll? Answer these questions about him.**

Who does Rudolf Rassendyll . . .
1 look like?
2 make friends with?
3 try to rescue?
4 fight against?
5 fall in love with?

2 **How much can you guess about this story? Choose words to complete this passage.**

The story happens in Ruritania, which *is* / *is not* a real place, and is both an *adventure* / *animal* story and a *crime* / *love* story. There will be a lot of *ghosts* / *fighting* in the Castle of Zenda, and in the end the King's *enemies* / *friends* will *rescue* / *kill* him. The story will end *happily* / *sadly* for the King, but *happily* / *sadly* for Rudolf Rassendyll.

3 **On the back cover of the book are these two questions. Can you guess the answers?**

1 Who will rescue the King from his enemies?
2 Who will win the heart of the beautiful Princess Flavia?

While Reading

Read Chapters 1 to 3. Who were these sentences said or written about?

1 'I know he can't do much about his hair, or his nose.'
2 The boy grew into a man with blue eyes, a long straight nose, and dark red hair.
3 'She's travelling on the same train as you, but don't fall in love with her.'
4 'He's only the second son and will never be king himself.'
5 'Friends who want the same place and the same wife.'
6 'Good heavens! He looks just like the King!'
7 'We've been trying to wake him for half an hour, but he's sleeping like a dead man.'
8 'God save them both.'

Read Chapters 4 to 6. Choose the best question-word for these questions, and then answer them.

How / What / When / Where / Who / Whose / Why
1 . . . faces did Rudolf remember from the coronation?
2 . . . did Rudolf and Sapt discover on their return to Zenda?
3 . . . did they go after the fight with the Duke's men?
4 . . . were the Six?
5 . . . did Rudolf feel about the Princess Flavia?
6 . . . did Antoinette de Mauban want to help Rudolf?
7 . . . did a tea-table help to save Rudolf's life?

Before you read Chapters 7, 8, and 9, can you guess what happens? Choose Y (yes) or N (no) for each of these ideas.

1 Rudolf asks Princess Flavia to marry him. Y/N
2 Rudolf tells the Princess who he really is. Y/N
3 Rudolf decides to kill the King and marry Flavia. Y/N
4 Duke Michael offers Rudolf a hundred thousand pounds
   to leave the country. Y/N

Read Chapters 7 to 9. Who said this, and to whom? Why did they say it? Match the sentences to the explanations below.

1 'I didn't love you before, but I do now.'
2 'You're the finest Elphberg of them all.'
3 'Don't go out unless you have six men or more with you!'
4 'Duke Michael doesn't understand men like us!'
5 'You'll still be King of Ruritania in a year's time.'

6 He thought Rudolf was a brave man, and a true gentleman.
7 He saw that he and Rudolf were the same, because they
   both loved adventure more than money.
8 She did not realize that he was not the same man.
9 He could not see any way of rescuing the real King.
10 He wanted to warn Rudolf that his life was in danger.

Read Chapters 10 and 11, then match these halves of sentences.

1 Rudolf swam around the castle to find the pipe . . .
2 Rudolf and his friends killed two of the Six that night, . . .
3 Rupert wanted Antoinette and hated Duke Michael, . . .
4 The plan was for Johann to take a note to Antoinette, . . .

5 At the same time, Johann would open the front door . . .
6 Rudolf would hide in the moat by the drawbridge, . . .
7 Before he left, Rudolf gave Flavia his family ring, . . .

8 telling her to scream for Duke Michael's help in the night.
9 and she promised to wear it for ever.
10 because Antoinette loved the Duke, and not him.
11 which went from the prisoner's room down into the moat.
12 and then enter the old castle and save the King.
13 but they also lost three of their own men.
14 in order to let Sapt and Fritz into the new castle.

Before you read Chapter 12, can you guess what will happen?

1 Will everything happen as Rudolf has planned?
2 Will Rudolf kill all of the Six, as he had promised?
3 Will Duke Michael die? If so, how?
4 Will Rudolf marry Flavia?

Read Chapters 12 and 13. Here are some untrue sentences about them. Rewrite them with the correct information.

1 When Antoinette screamed, there was no one in her room.
2 Johann did not come, so Sapt and Fritz could not get in through the castle door.
3 Duke Michael killed Antoinette, so Rupert of Hentzau tried to shoot the Duke.
4 Rudolf killed the other four of the Six.
5 Rudolf and Rupert fought wildly, and Rupert was killed.
6 Flavia married Rudolf Rassendyll, and forgot the King.

After Reading

1 **Who was who in this story? Complete the sentences with the right names. Then rewrite the sentences as a paragraph about each person, using pronouns (*he, she*, etc.) and linking words (*and, but, who, so, because*, etc.) where possible.**

Duke Michael / Princess Flavia / Antoinette de Mauban / Rudolf Rassendyll / Rupert of Hentzau

1 _____ was a young Ruritanian nobleman.

2 _____ was a beautiful French lady.

3 _____ was a young English nobleman.

4 _____ was the King's beautiful cousin.

5 _____ was the King's half-brother.

6 _____ had the Elphberg hair and nose.

7 _____ was a wild and dangerous fighter.

8 _____ loved Duke Michael.

9 _____ wanted to be the King and to marry Flavia.

10 _____ fell in love with Rudolf Rassendyll.

11 _____ tried to kill Rudolf Rassendyll several times.

12 _____ looked just like the King.

13 _____ kept the King a prisoner in the Castle of Zenda.

14 _____ knew she could not marry Rudolf Rassendyll.

15 _____ didn't want Duke Michael to become king and marry Flavia.

16 _____ was one of Duke Michael's men.

17 _____ agreed to take the King's place.

18 _____ planned to kill the King if anyone tried to rescue him.
19 _____ had to marry the King.
20 _____ killed the Duke in a fight about Antoinette.
21 _____ tried to help Rudolf Rassendyll rescue the King.
22 _____ wanted the chance of a great adventure.
23 _____ was killed by one of his own men in the end.

2 There are 15 words from the story hidden in this word search. Find the words, and draw lines through them. (The words go from left to right, and from top to bottom.)

H	D	A	G	G	E	R	E	D	L	L
K	P	S	W	I	M	R	M	R	C	A
N	C	E	M	I	C	O	H	A	O	D
I	A	M	O	A	T	P	A	W	U	D
F	S	E	L	R	U	E	P	B	S	E
E	T	K	I	S	S	E	R	R	I	R
T	L	O	W	I	N	E	F	I	N	R
H	E	E	S	W	O	R	D	D	N	I
R	E	V	O	L	V	E	R	G	T	N
Z	A	P	R	I	S	O	N	E	U	G

Now write down all the letters that don't have lines through them. Begin with the first line and go across each line to the end. You will have 28 letters, which will make 6 words.

1 What are the words?
2 Who told which person to say these words, and why?
3 Why was Rudolf surprised when he heard them?

3 **What did Sapt tell Princess Flavia about Rudolf at the end of the story? Put their conversation in the right order, and write in the speakers' names. Sapt speaks first (number 6).**

1 _____ 'Yes, we think he had. So Rassendyll took the King's place at the coronation, and we planned to bring the King back to Strelsau that night.'

2 _____ 'His name, your Highness, is Rudolf Rassendyll.'

3 _____ 'Gone? Gone where?'

4 _____ 'I'll explain. On coronation day the King lay in Zenda like a dead man, after he had drunk a bottle of Duke Michael's wine the night before.'

5 _____ 'But you didn't bring him back.'

6 _____ 'It's true, your Highness. He is not the King. He is an Englishman, a visitor to our country.'

7 _____ 'And is the King still a prisoner?'

8 _____ 'No, your Highness, we didn't. When we returned to Zenda at midnight, the King had gone.'

9 _____ 'Brave . . . and kind and loving. Oh Sapt! How can I live without him?'

10 _____ 'No, his Majesty is now free, and his enemies are dead – thanks to a brave young Englishman.'

11 _____ 'Ah, the Rassendyll family . . . of course. But I still don't understand. Why did he pretend to be the King?'

12 _____ 'Duke Michael had taken him to the Castle of Zenda, as his prisoner.'

13 _____ 'Duke Michael had put something in the wine?'

14 _____ 'An Englishman? How can that be? He has the red hair, the Elphberg nose . . . Sapt, who is he?'

4 Perhaps this is what some of the people in the story were thinking. Who were they, and where were they at the time? Complete their thoughts in your own words. (Use as many words as you like.)

1 'I don't believe this! Here he is, walking into the church, when he should be still asleep. Didn't _____?'

2 'Everyone's watching us as we dance, but I don't care. When he looks into my eyes like that, I _____.'

3 'He's playing the lover very well, but – Good heavens! He's going to tell her who he really is! I _____!'

4 'I knew he'd refuse the money. But my dagger nearly got him. And now I must ride hard – his men _____.'

5 'He's killed the only man I loved! And he's just standing there, laughing at me. I'm _____!'

6 'I'm still worried about him. Since his walking holiday in Austria he's been so quiet, so sad. Perhaps _____.'

7 'It's been five years now. The same rose, the same message – and he can't wait to see them. Will _____?'

5 Here are some different endings for the story. Which do you prefer, or do you like the ending in the book best? Why?

- Flavia decides not to marry the King. She marries Rudolf, and goes to live quietly with him in England.
- After Rupert of Hentzau escapes from Antoinette's room, he runs back to the old castle and kills the King before Rudolf can stop him. Rudolf becomes King of Ruritania.
- Ten years later the King dies. Rudolf Rassendyll returns to Ruritania and marries Flavia.

ABOUT THE AUTHOR

Anthony Hope is the pen-name of Sir Anthony Hope Hawkins. He was born in London in 1863, and studied at Marlborough School, and then Balliol College, Oxford. At Oxford he was President of the Union, and he received a first-class degree. In 1887 Hope began work as a lawyer. He wrote stories in his free time, and in 1890 he published his first novel, *A Man of Mark*. Then one day in November 1893 he was walking back from work, when the idea of 'Ruritania' came into his head. The next day he wrote the first chapter of *The Prisoner of Zenda*, and one month later the story was finished. The book appeared in April 1894, and was an immediate success. Hope then became a full-time writer, publishing many popular novels, plays, and short stories. His second Ruritanian novel, *Rupert of Hentzau* (1898), follows the continuing adventures of Rudolf Rassendyll. Anthony Hope died in 1933.

The Prisoner of Zenda has appeared in many languages, and found success in many different countries. There have been a number of theatre versions of the story, and at least five films. The finest of these is probably David O. Selznik's 1937 film, starring Ronald Colman and Douglas Fairbanks. The story is as popular today as it was a hundred years ago, and is still one of the world's best-loved adventure stories.

ABOUT BOOKWORMS

OXFORD BOOKWORMS LIBRARY
Classics • True Stories • Fantasy & Horror • Human Interest
Crime & Mystery • Thriller & Adventure

The OXFORD BOOKWORMS LIBRARY offers a wide range of original and adapted stories, both classic and modern, which take learners from elementary to advanced level through six carefully graded language stages:

Stage 1 (400 headwords)	**Stage 4** (1400 headwords)
Stage 2 (700 headwords)	**Stage 5** (1800 headwords)
Stage 3 (1000 headwords)	**Stage 6** (2500 headwords)

More than fifty titles are also available on cassette, and there are many titles at Stages 1 to 4 which are specially recommended for younger learners. In addition to the introductions and activities in each Bookworm, resource material includes photocopiable test worksheets and Teacher's Handbooks, which contain advice on running a class library and using cassettes, and the answers for the activities in the books.

Several other series are linked to the OXFORD BOOKWORMS LIBRARY. They range from highly illustrated readers for young learners, to playscripts, non-fiction readers, and unsimplified texts for advanced learners.

Oxford Bookworms Starters	*Oxford Bookworms Factfiles*
Oxford Bookworms Playscripts	*Oxford Bookworms Collection*

Details of these series and a full list of all titles in the OXFORD BOOKWORMS LIBRARY can be found in the *Oxford English* catalogues. A selection of titles from the OXFORD BOOKWORMS LIBRARY can be found on the next pages.

Kidnapped

ROBERT LOUIS STEVENSON

Retold by Clare West

'I ran to the side of the ship. "Help, help! Murder!" I screamed, and my uncle slowly turned to look at me. I did not see any more. Already strong hands were pulling me away. Then something hit my head; I saw a great flash of fire, and fell to the ground . . .'

And so begin David Balfour's adventures. He is kidnapped, taken to sea, and meets many dangers. He also meets a friend, Alan Breck. But Alan is in danger himself, on the run from the English army across the wild Highlands of Scotland . . .

The Crown of Violet

GEOFFREY TREASE

Retold by John Escott

High up on a stone seat in the great open-air theatre of Athens, Alexis, son of Leon, watches the Festival of Plays – and dreams of seeing his own play on that famous stage.

So, as the summer passes, Alexis writes his play for the next year's Festival. But then, with his friend Corinna, he learns that Athens has enemies – enemies who do not like Athenian democracy, and who are planning a revolution to end it all . . .

On the Edge

GILLIAN CROSS

Retold by Clare West

When Tug wakes up, he is not in his own bedroom at home. The door is locked and there are bars across the window. Loud music hammers through the house and through his head. Then a woman comes in and says that she is his mother, but Tug knows that she is *not* his mother . . .

Outside, Jinny stares through the trees at the lonely house on the hill. She hears strange noises, but she turns away. After all, it's none of her business . . .

Skyjack!

TIM VICARY

When a large plane is hijacked, the Prime Minister looks at the list of passengers and suddenly becomes very, very frightened.

There is a name on the list that the Prime Minister knows very well – too well. There is someone on that plane who will soon be dead – if the hijackers can find out who he is!

And there isn't much time. One man lies dead on the runway. In a few minutes the hijackers will use their guns again. And the Prime Minister knows who they are going to kill.

Wyatt's Hurricane

DESMOND BAGLEY

Retold by Jennifer Bassett

Hurricane Mabel is far out in the Atlantic Ocean and moving slowly northwards. Perhaps it will never come near land at all. But if it hits the island of San Fernandez, many thousands of people will die. There could be winds of more than 250 kilometres an hour. There could be a huge tidal wave from the sea, which will drown the capital city of St Pierre. Mabel will destroy houses, farms, roads, bridges . . .

Only one man, David Wyatt, believes that Mabel will hit San Fernandez, but nobody will listen to him . . .

Treasure Island

ROBERT LOUIS STEVENSON

Retold by John Escott

'Suddenly, there was a high voice screaming in the darkness: "Pieces of eight! Pieces of eight! Pieces of eight!" It was Long John Silver's parrot, Captain Flint! I turned to run . . .'

But young Jim Hawkins does not escape from the pirates this time. Will he and his friends find the treasure before the pirates do? Will they escape from the island, and sail back to England with a ship full of gold?